Businesspeople Don't Like to Read, We Scan

A Quick, Strategic Guide for Effective Business
Writing

By

Al Golzari

Book 2 of 2 in Speaking and Writing Series

Please subscribe to my YouTube channel: Al Golzari

Check out my videos on presentation skills, business writing, and many more topics.

Send in comments and questions and I'll answer them in an upcoming Q&A video. And you'll get a **chance to win** a paperback copy of my presentation skills book:

It's Called Presenting, Not Talking Out Loud: A Quick, Strategic Guide to Effective Presentations

INTRODUCTION

This book is a complement to my first book on presentation skills, *It's Called Presenting, Not Talking Out Loud: A Quick, Strategic Guide on Effective Presentations*.

Let me first get this out of the way. I know some authors write a companion book where you've already purchased the first book and the companion is at least half (or more) the same. This is NOT the case here. I promise. With maybe one exception of half a page (where I make mention of it), there's no duplication. That's not cool. And I wouldn't do that to you.

In some ways, I shouldn't have written this book. I really don't have the "right" to write a book on writing, since I'm a pretty awful writer (I really am). I'm a talker, not a writer.

But...in many ways, I'm precisely the one to write this book. This book is about business writing – something I've become pretty decent at over the past decade or so, mainly based on my industry experience.

If I was a good writer, all around, I wouldn't have appreciated the specific nature of business writing. And I would have taken all of this, for granted.

Business writing is different than almost every other type of writing for one main reason:

Business writing is about results, ultimately.

In other words, where other types of writing may take you on a journey of some kind...some wonderful, mystical journey, business writing doesn't have much appetite for the journey.

We believe in the destination. Give us the destination and if we want to know any parts of the journey, we will ask.

It really does boil down to the above.

Business professionals and executives are too busy to bother with details (at least at first). They need the bottom-line deliverables presented UPFRONT.

And what you do in business writing, whatever type of document it may be, is to be:

- Clear
- Concise
- Consistent

The more you can adjust your style to bullet points, the MORE EFFECTIVE you'll be as a written communicator and PEOPLE WILL NOTICE and appreciate this style. Please trust me on this. You can even get some type of competitive advantage by doing this.

These advantages can lead to:

- More opportunities for projects
- A "trusted advisor," as we like to say in industry
- Greater chances at promotions

And honestly, you'll also be regarded as someone who's more intelligent, experienced...seasoned.
I guarantee that if you follow these principles, you'll have a great chance at all of the above.

I'm rooting for you...

WHO THIS GUIDEBOOK IS FOR

Granted, this guide is a bit more basic than my book on presentation skills and therefore it's more suited for graduate and undergraduate students, as well as businesspeople still early on in their careers.

At the same time, this guide can work well for people who may not be in industry, per se, but need to prepare documentation related to business. As well as more experienced businesspeople who may need some refreshers or further guidance.

The guide was written in a way to cover most issues. From specific ones such as writing a proposal, or very general ones such as how to change your writing style in emails. And many things in between.

The goal has been to create a guidebook that cuts out all of the fat and unnecessary theory for those who just need the keys.

If you're a student enrolled in a communications course or perhaps a business writing course, etc., my hope is that you can treat this guidebook as a supplement to the other materials your instructor has assigned. And it's my sincere hope that some instructors would adopt this guide as part of their curriculum.

I wanted to simplify and make this as practical and user-friendly as possible. As with all texts, you can read this from start to finish, and I hope since there aren't many pages, you'll find it all concise and useful. If you were to read this from start to finish, it's probably about a 90-minute read. However, you can also specifically flip to what you may need.

TABLE OF CONTENTS

This guide is divided into two parts: strategy and execution.

STRATEGY:

EXECUTION:

CHAPTER ONE | DON'T MAKE PEOPLE READ

CHAPTER PURPOSE:
- To provide the importance of brevity and organization in business writing and set up the overall theme of this book.

I once gave the CFO of a company I was working at a deck I prepared. Before I walked her through it, the first thing I said was: "So the good news, this entire walk through is only two slides."

She genuinely smiled and looked happy (and perhaps even relieved).

The most important part of this book is this:

In business writing, do NOT make your reader (audience) READ!

In business, we don't like to read. We don't. We like to scan, at best. And that's on a "good" day. Allow your reader to SCAN and LOOK. Not read. And yes, I'm well aware of the irony of giving you this advice by asking you to ~~read~~, I mean SCAN it!

There are a few reasons for this:

1. People in business don't have the time
2. People in business don't have the patience

As it relates to point 2, I'm allowed to say this, being in industry. Businesspeople really don't have all that much patience. And the more experienced and older businesspeople get, the less patience they have.

If you're in your twenties within perhaps five or so years' experience, there's a good chance that you've come across a good amount of emails from senior managers (VP and above) and have been puzzled as to why their grammar is so "terrible."

On the one hand, you're right. Their grammar is really terrible. It's not that there are misspellings, per se. It's more about leaving out words that you wouldn't leave out, not using a period at the end of a sentence, and just a bunch of fragmented sentences and/or phrases.

But in principle, the reason why they write that way is because they're well experienced and understand the VIRTUE of brevity and focusing on the point. And that's why their writing skills, from a traditional standpoint, are "poor." But in some ways, their writing style is brilliant.

As I said in the introduction, people in industry don't like to be taken on a journey. Give us the destination. I mean, in general, what's better? Telling me your wonderful vacation to wherever you went? Or how you got there?

You'll be SURPRISED how many people waste time by telling others how they got there.

Of course, there are some exceptions and situations that I want to be mindful and respectful of. But professions such as law are NOT business professions. So attorneys, paralegals, etc., don't count here.

When you prepare almost any type of business document, either as an email or a report, deck, etc., make sure that you write it with the above in mind.

Do your absolute best to get to your main point as upfront as possible. This doesn't necessarily mean you want to constantly use tactics that are "brochure-like." There may be some room for that, at times. And there are some types of documents that I'll be discussing in this book where that would make sense.

But when you're writing to your boss, for example, skip the sensationalism. It's not about that.

The beauty (yes, beauty) of embracing this is that when you write clearly and effectively, your reader will want to KEEP reading more. When you do a poor job at getting your point across, not only will your reader not want to read anything at all, but they'll stop prematurely and won't come back to it.

It's from this foundation that I decided to write this quick book. I had no initial plans of writing this book, or my book on presentation skills. They both just happened naturally.

I'll be covering some of the key issues that I think students as well as younger professionals can use to their advantage. Such as one-pagers, getting to your point faster, using the direct method of communication, etc.

ORGANIZATION

As you begin to improve your business writing skills, this will all become more naturally to you. Along with how you'll want to organize your documents and emails.

While you can organize your emails and documents in several effective ways, the idea is to make sure you do it in a way (especially for emails that have a lot of info) where people can literally run their eyes through the document and then focus on whatever they feel is necessary.

The organization of your document and the elements I've included in this example are many of the issues we'll tackle in this guidebook.

Take a look at this email I sent to business partners, which was admittedly a bit long. Sometimes long emails are necessary. But, you can "ease the pain" by organizing them and making them much easier to digest.

Please read the following email and then I'll dissect how and why I organized it this way.

Dear Business Partners:

I want to sincerely thank you for participating in this year's program. We're very appreciative of your interest and participation. I'll be guiding this project - and a very short bio about me is at the end of this email.

Project Criteria
I've created a new document that should help with some general criteria for the project, in the event some clients are still formulating project ideas.

Initial Steps – Client Profile Sheet
- We've created a Client Profile Sheet, that I believe will help define each of your projects and ensure that we are aligned with expectations.
- Please be assured that all information that you provide will be kept in strict confidence. If there is a need, at the onset or anytime throughout the project, to share information or documents that you prefer are protected with a signed NDA, we

will be happy to accommodate. Feel free to send me those requests.

Initial Client Profile Sheet: Requested Turn-Around – Dec. 15

- If you can begin to fill out the Client Profile Sheets (one sheet per project, please, if you have multiple projects) which will be in your dedicated Google shared drive and upload these back to your Google shared drive by **Dec. 15**, that would be most appreciated.
- That way you and I can have some dialogue and a chance to tighten up any projects/scope.
- Of course, feel free to treat these sheets as fluid, living documents, for now.
- Throughout the project, we will continue to add any relevant documents to the shared drives (such as a project milestone sheet and other documents, that we intend to have students update bi-weekly) and feel free to do so as well.

General Process

There will be more detailed communication, as needed. But the general process for this course will typically look like this:

1. You and I finalize the client profile sheets by around Jan. 15, if not sooner.

2. During the first week I will create "project shells" where I'll just offer the industry but not the actual company. Once their choices are finalized, I'll reveal the actual company names.
3. I'll ask participants to create a quick profile sheet (see blank, attached) where they will fill this out and place on your specific shared drive as members of your client team.
4. I will divide the course into separate phases with defined milestones for them to achieve and all necessary documentation will be shared with you.
5. As far as communication between you and participants throughout the semester, please see directly below.
6. I'd like to set up a mid-semester touch base between you and each participant group. *This can be done via Skype of Facetime, etc.
7. The final presentations will be a formal presentation along with a formal report to follow. Timing will be first two weeks of May.
8. If there are any suggestions you have to the above, general process, I'm open to your ideas or concerns. Please let me know.

Point of Contact with Your Company/Communication and Ours

- If you can please think about a main point of contact for the semester, that would be great.
- As for participants asking questions, if there are very "obvious" questions that I can answer for

them, I will. But for questions that I don't know (obviously) or questions that I may know, I will encourage them to ask you; it's part of their learning process.
- I will ask the participants to get in the habit of asking initial questions only about once a week in order for you not to be overwhelmed; we know you're very busy.

Logistics
- To hopefully create the easiest and most efficient experience for you, we've created a Google drive where shared documents will live and each of you and our assigned student groups can have easy access to files, at any time.
- You will be given access to the drive momentarily and should receive a notification soon.

Contact
Feel free to reach out to me at any time with any questions. I'm available via email or cell phone at any time.

Thank you again for your participation. I look forward to working with all of you for a rewarding experience. And on behalf of the team, the opportunities that you're providing here will surely create an impactful experience as they start their careers, and help prepare them for real-world scenarios.

Best, Al

Bio

Al Golzari is a senior-level product development, innovation, sourcing, and vendor management professional with 15+ years' experience in the retailing/consumer products industry - with experience in international markets on the front- and back-end. And adjunct instructor of marketing, international marketing/business, innovation, entrepreneurship, and business communication. Successful roles at Limited Brands, Macy's, and Target, among others. Significant experience in international business, including international product strategy and off-shore sourcing and vendor management. BA in Sociology from New York University; MBA in Marketing from Fairleigh Dickinson University.

Now that you've read the email, let me dissect this for you.

Many people have the natural tendency to introduce themselves in the beginning, and I completely understand that. But even though you're writing this email to people who don't know you yet, the email is not about you. At the same time, you do deserve (and it's warranted) to share a little something about yourself and credentials. The way I tackled this is to put a small bio at the end. And make a quick mention of this in the first paragraph. I think this tactic generally works.

The next thing I did was think about all of the things I need to discuss in the email. And then I put them (mentally) into "buckets." And gave each a name, as you saw above, in bold (with one exception, see below):

- *Project Criteria*
- *Initial Steps – Client Profile Sheet*
- *Initial Client Profile Sheet: Requested Turn-Around – Dec. 15*
- *General Process*
- *Point of Contact with Your Company/Communication and Ours*
- *Logistics*
- *Contact*
- *Bio*

The first thing I'd say about the above buckets is that, as you can probably decipher for yourself, are in some general type of chronological order. And that's what I'd recommend for you, in general. Of course, there are exceptions. There's one element above that has a hard-date request, but your elements don't need to necessarily have a date associated with them, to be in chronological order.

The chronological order can be date-driven or simply what you "naturally" need your readers to know or do first. In other words, what makes the most natural sense in terms of the overall project.

Within each bucket (with the exception of the bio), you'll notice I made sure I used either bullet points or numbered points, which there is a chapter devoted to in this book.

It's very important, in business writing, to put as many things as you can (that make sense) in bulletized or numbered form. It makes people absorb the content so much easier. Again, the idea is to not make your readers READ, but instead, scan.

The one bucket that I used numbers instead of buckets was *General Process*. I did that because, again, whether it's date-driven or not, for the most part the information I needed to share in that section does have some natural order to it, to a large extent.

Lastly, I wanted to touch upon why each bucket was placed in bold with the exception of the *Bio*. Again, as mentioned, the email is not about me and I didn't want it to come across that way. So I italicized but didn't bold *Bio*, to help reinforce that I wasn't trying to make it about myself.
Granted there may be some subtlety to that sort of thing, but personally, I thought it was a nice touch. It's similar to how some people always close an email

by not capitalizing their name. You'll notice about 20% of people overall close their emails with their last name like this:

Best,
janet

So that's all, it's just a stylistic issue.

CHAPTER TWO | PLEASE GET TO THE POINT FASTER

- To use the direct method in business writing and share with your reader UPFRONT what the purpose of your message is.
- To put supporting and background info, as it may relate, afterwards.

If you sent me a simple email asking me what my favorite movie is, you're probably waiting for a reply with, more or less, the name of the movie, right? OK, maybe I can offer a little "extra" than a one-liner. Maybe I can tell you my favorite movie is and <u>why</u>. That's fair *enough*.

BUT...what if I began replying to your email this way:

There are many wonderful movies out there, in so many different genres. There are dramas, comedies, action, horror, etc.

These genres can make us laugh, cry (sometimes in a good way), find inspiration, keep us on edge, etc....

See where I'm going with this?

Now how about if I wrote you back with one simple word?

Scarface.

Do you hopefully see the difference?!

In the first scenario, I'm doing what? I'm taking you on that journey that I asked you to avoid in the introduction and the first chapter.

In the second scenario, I'm offering you the destination. Plain and simple. Nice and clean. No fuss, no muss.

In the second scenario, I didn't philosophize. By the way, I did mention it was fair *enough* if I told you why Scarface was my favorite movie. BUT at the same time, remember, did you ask me for the why? You actually didn't. Which is another lesson, in and of itself. Offer people what they've asked for. No more, no less.

OK, so what am I driving at with this chapter? In the first scenario, this is what so many business students (undergrad AND grad), as well as my business associates who are in their twenties and early thirties, do to me all the time! ☺

And, umm, no offense, it drives me mad!

Over the years I've read so many emails that were well-meaning, but were far too long and didn't get to the point fast enough.

When sending emails, do your best to state what it is you're asking for/trying to achieve, upfront. As opposed to providing far too much of a backstory. And make sure you're clear.

I've received many emails like this. And this is not an exaggeration. **What you see in bold is my emphasis:**

Hi Al:

I'm originally from Florida. That's where my family still lives and I moved up here a few years ago when I started school.

I'll be heading down to Florida for the holidays and I had booked my ticket a long time ago, to get the lowest price possible.

I didn't realize, at the time, and this is my fault, that the final exam is scheduled the day after I leave for vacation.

*At this point, if I were to change my ticket, it would be very expensive and I can't afford it right now. I'm really sorry. **Is there anything I can do to take the final exam at a different time?***

OK, so no offense, but this email is not written in the most effective and concise way. Here's how I think it can be better written:

Hi Al:
Is there anything I can do to take the final exam at a different time?

I'll be heading down to Florida for the holidays and I had booked my ticket a long time ago, to get the lowest price possible. At this point, if I were to change my ticket, it would be very expensive and I can't afford it right now.

I didn't realize, at the time, and this is my fault, that the final exam is scheduled the day after I leave for vacation. I'm really sorry.

If you noticed, I didn't change the structure of the sentences and I didn't change the words. I'm not providing a grammar lesson here. I'm sure many of you are much stronger writers than me (I'm a talker, not a writer). But I did two things:

1.Took out some information that isn't necessary. And I'm sorry that you may find it slightly offensive that I recommend taking out the part about you being from Florida, and your family living there. I'm not trying to be cruel and non-human. But you're going on vacation, and it's just not relevant. If this was, unfortunately, a funeral you needed to attend, then maybe the info about where you're from is a bit more relevant. **See my point?** But it's not a situation like that, and whether you're going to Florida, California, or wherever, it doesn't matter.

2.Rearranged information so that you state what you're asking for – <u>upfront</u>. And the reader can get to your point – <u>faster</u>.

Most people, especially in the business world, do NOT LIKE TO READ. No, I'm being serious.

In the business world, we don't like to read. We like to scan. And then when there is something to read after we scan, fine.

But we want to scan, to get the gist of the message and its main point. And that's all we need.

If you want to look at all of this a different way, this is sometimes referred to the direct vs. indirect communication style – which can apply to both presentations (see my Presentations book) as well as writing. It's a very simple concept.

But in business writing, unless you're playing a more specific role in the organization, most if not all, of your writing should be the **direct method**.

The direct method teaches us to offer your conclusion first. I totally get it, often times we need to offer some context or some type of justification on why we are offering a particular conclusion. Fine! Put it afterwards. Here's a fictitious example, but one that happens to me often. One of my supervisors may send me an email asking me something like this:

Hi Al:
Wanted to know how you felt about giving a presentation on the highlights of your most recent sourcing trip to China. I brought up your trip in a meeting this morning and the EVP seemed pretty interested in learning more. I know it's already Thursday and the presentation would need to happen next Tuesday. Let me know your thoughts!
Thanks,
Stacie

So here's how many people might reply to this email. And admittedly, I used to write like this as well:

Hi Stacie:
That's great to hear! Yes, it would be a little tight in terms of timing. And I'd also feel better if you and I had a quick touch base on what you think I should present. I want to be specific as possible and would prefer if I had a gauge to know how general or in-depth I should make it. Maybe we can connect on

that tomorrow (Friday) or Monday morning at the latest?
Thanks,
Al

Now, is my email above to Stacie the worst in the world? Probably not, and I probably didn't commit any crimes here. But, it's still not that great, to be honest. It can be better. Here's one way:

Hi Stacie:
That's great to hear! ***Yes, I'd be happy to do it and can commit to it.*** *Can we have a quick touch base on what you think I should present? I want to be specific as possible and would prefer if I had a gauge to know how general or in-depth I should make it. Can we connect on that tomorrow (Friday) or Monday morning at the latest?*
Thanks,
Al

I think this is better.

First, look at what's in bold: **the conclusion**. The email has a few details in it and some language that is accommodating and deferential, yet the bottom line is that this is a typical business email and it's asking me one thing.

Can I do a presentation next Tuesday for the EVP? The answer to that question is yes or no. That's it. Not maybe. So what you see in bold is answering Stacie's question upfront. She doesn't have to "hunt" for it.

I provided a quick "That's great to hear!" (in both scenarios) upfront because I want to quickly show my enthusiasm and appreciation. But in the second scenario I immediately answered her question. And yes, I had some questions myself, but I posed those after.

Second, look at the slightly different language in the second scenario. They are mainly the same questions but in the second scenario I posed them a little more confidently, as you can hopefully see in my tone. Since I committed to doing it, my tone has changed. I'm projecting more confidence and I'm providing my boss more confidence. In the first scenario, I'm also a bit wishy-washy.

My boss is expecting an answer that's either yes or no. She's not looking for wishy-washy.

So for the most part, in your business communication, use the direct method. Provide the reader the answer first, and then provide whatever supporting info that's necessary, afterwards.

Yes, of course you can say things such as "How are you?", etc. I'm not trying to tell you to be cold, ha! But don't offer info that, quite frankly, your reader doesn't want or need. It's one of those things that they'll appreciate it, even if it's not always evident.

CHAPTER THREE | "FYI" WRITING VS. PERSUASIVE WRITING

CHAPTER PURPOSE:
- To understand the difference between wanting a reply, by making a call to action vs. a more simple "for your information" type message.
- To develop your skills and confidence in directly and explicitly stating what you may want to happen as a result of your message.

If you haven't experienced this yet, many people write emails where they hope to receive some type of substantive reply. And it doesn't happen. Either there's no reply, or, at best, the reply is benign. I need to share this with you because this used to be one of my main problems when I'd send business emails in the past. Until I figured out what I was doing wrong.

Continuing with the theme that businesspeople are busy, when you send emails that you want some type of meaningful reply to, make sure you don't send them in an "FYI" tone.

Now sure, there are some emails that you'll send that are truly an FYI. Maybe it's some interesting business article you read and want to pass along.

But if you're looking for a reply, make sure, in some way, **you ask for one**.

Typically, when you ask for some type of reply, you're most likely being persuasive. Or you should be persuasive. In some way.

In persuasive writing, there needs to be some type of "call to action," as I always like to say.

Please don't assume that persuasion is essentially offering your opinions. Some people have some trouble understanding the difference between opinions and persuasion. They are related, for sure. But are different things.

Sometimes just a subtle difference to the "untrained" eye. But a difference, for sure.

And this definitely has a direct bearing on whether people see your business emails as an "FYI" or if they'll be propelled to do – something.

Opinions are statements that you hold strong - or even true. And they are backed up by a range of facts and also possibly, emotions. And that's fine.

The problem is that sometimes, even people with a good amount of experience, put too much emphasis on their opinion as their persuasion strategy. When you're either the direct recipient of this, or on an email as a cc, believe me, you'll see their email come across in an unprofessional and "too" emotional way.

Persuasion is a **different** mechanism. While you may use, of course, your opinions and perspective in persuasive writing, please remember the difference is that in persuasive business writing you're asking someone to DO SOMETHING. And that "something" that you want them to do – helps THEM and/or the COMPANY, etc., in some way. You want something to happen.

Example:
Opinion: The XYZ legislation will officially become law starting on Feb. 1. It's the first time we've had real reform in this area. It can change the way we look at our business.

In the above, there are facts and also some opinion. Aside from that, where is the persuasion? I don't see it.

In business writing, we can't "hope" that the above is enough for the reader to do something. We need to actively do, not passively wait.

Let's look at the example again, a little differently.

Persuasion: The XYZ legislation will officially become law starting on Feb. 1. It's the first time we've had real reform in this area. **We have an opportunity to create a new set of competitive advantages that we need to implement over the next six months in order to take advantage of the new laws and mitigate direct competition.** *Over lunch sometime this week, I'd like to present our plan of action for the next 3 months.*

I hope that in the above, you see this as more persuasive. I've added what I think is important, in bold.

When you're writing anything in your business life that you want a response to, make sure that you're EXPLICIT about it with some type of call to action.

FANCY WORDS

I figured I'd throw this into this chapter; not to use fancy words. If you've read my book on presentation skills, this was in there, too.

Too many young people think fancy words are good to use. They're not. They're pretentious.

Use <u>conversational</u> language whenever you can. For example, instead of saying something like:

One must consider the ramifications of...

Try something like:

This is important because...

This is a better way of not only being more "real" but also less distant.

I'd also recommend, as appropriate, not to use "$50 words" when a "$5 word" will do just fine. I'm sure you've heard this before, but it's true.

I'm not suggesting lowering the caliber of your vocabulary. What I'm saying is, **don't use a steak knife to cut butter.**

- Why use "nefarious" if "evil" will do just fine?
- Why say "ascertain" if "figure out" works just as effectively?

Actually, "evil," depending on your topic, may be a more descriptive word and better convey your meaning, anyway.

I hate to do this, but I'm going to reference politicians. In general, voters resonate more with candidates who use "plain English." Use fancy words when it's called for. In most cases though, don't overdo it.

CHAPTER FOUR | PROPOSALS AND PITCHES

CHAPTER PURPOSE:
- To better understand that proposals and pitches need to focus on why the reader should care and the benefit to them. And less about making it about you/your organization.
- To organize your proposals and pitches in an easier to digest style.

So there's something I need to get out there, right out of the gate. If you've experienced this like I have, your alumni association of where you went to college will send you a letter approximately once or twice a year asking for donations. (Students who are still undergrads, don't worry, they're coming).

What is the number one issue with these donation requests?

The problem is there's too much emphasis on the school and not enough emphasis on you, the alum.

There's something you may have heard before (I'm pretty sure) but we still seem to forget: WIIFT?

What's in it for them (the audience)? Or in this case, as the recipient of the letter, what's in it for you?

Unless you do a good job in explaining what's in it for people, **most people don't care**. It's a truth of life. Do you get excited when you get a donation letter from your alma mater?

You need to put the emphasis there. You really do. Of course, have a balance and tell people about you and your organization. But ultimately, remember what you're marching to.

These letters put far too much emphasis on the school and what they're currently doing. Sorry, but it's true. Sometimes they'll showcase a particular student. No offense to those students, by the way.

There's more than one way to skin a cat, as they say. And more than one way to write a proposal. But there are some elements that all proposals should generally have:

- Summary (doesn't have to be an executive summary, as I discuss in a separate chapter)
- The problem, or situation
- The reason why this problem/situation exists
- Solution
- Budget
- Timing

In general, try and make your proposals no longer than two pages. If your proposal can fit on one page and it's not too crammed, great (see the chapter on the one-pager). But two pages is also acceptable. I try to not go over two pages on every proposal I've ever written. I'll offer two types of examples for you.

Here's one example that's written a bit differently and is more comprehensive than the one that follows. After you read this example, I'll break it down for you.

Dear Max:

Odyssey Group is an exciting company devoted to driving transformative social change throughout the world. Since 1987, we have identified and funded emerging entrepreneurs in over 40 countries. Some of our alumni have created some of the world's leading public service organizations as Echoing Green fellows, such as:

- City Year and Teach for America in the United States
- Appropriate Infrastructure Development Group in South America
- African Leadership Academy in Africa

Your organization, **The Max Foundation**, is the unquestioned leader in funding educational and healthcare opportunities in emerging nations, fully living up to its mission to "foster change through programs that are practical, financially sustainable, and results-oriented."

We at Odyssey Group have a proven track record of investing in quality people who deliver exceptional businesses that will help **The Max Foundation** grow into the next century and beyond.

What investing in Odyssey Group does?
- Ending Poverty in rural Kenya...by training women to produce, harvest, and bring to market quality fresh eggs.
- Maximize innovations and technology to expand access to justice and law to under-served communities in Uganda by...offering free legal assistance through mobile, online, seminars, and in-person consultations.
- Drive transparency and civic engagement to decrease water pollution in China by... training a youth-led water testing network and launching an interactive platform to motivate clean water solutions.

But we need The Max Foundation's help.

A gift from **you** will continue our successes when expanding into for-profit entrepreneurs.

We are seeking a minimum of $500,000 from **The Max Foundation** as a gift towards our for-profit expansion. With this investment, we will be able to fund our first round of for-profit entrepreneurs, giving them access to a proven network of successful business leaders throughout multiple industries. We currently function as an angel investor, funding entrepreneurs in their first round of financing through fellowships. While this has been an effective strategy for us, we know that we can do more.

And we need you now, more than ever.
What will your money do?
- Increase the number of fellows per year
- Facilitate the longevity of funding for fellows
- Provide coaching and support for fellows
- Develop new programs

I know firsthand the advantages Odyssey Group provides young entrepreneurs. When I was selected as a fellow in 1992, I was able to grow my business, helping inner city families gain health care, without having to worry about where my next funding was coming from. For the young entrepreneur, this is invaluable. We support this community of visionaries as they develop new solutions to society's toughest problems.

I would like to set up a face to face meeting with you to discuss this in person; if you would prefer to look at a complete proposal, I can have that sent to you at your earliest convenience.

Thank you for your consideration of this request. Your gift will be transformative to both our organizations and future entrepreneurs.

Together, I know we can drive real social change and move the needle.

Sincerely,
Al Golzari
President, Odyssey Group

To break this down a bit, this letter is mainly about The Max Foundation. If course, you're talking about yourself and trying to sell yourself. You have to. But the focus is on the client you're pitching to.

As you'll hopefully see, in one way or another I've covered the six elements discussed prior to the example: Summary; Problem; Rationale (Reason); Solution; Budget; Timing.

I was specific, explicit, and ultimately, my letter has a "call to action." And I'm not afraid to ask for it.

Example 2: Teaching Assistant Proposal

Teaching Assistant Proposal
Course: Marketing Capstone
Term/Duration: Spring 2020
Prepared by: Al Golzari

Description of Need/Overview: Marketing Capstone is a high-level, senior year undergraduate capstone with live client projects, divided among groups. Group sizes are typically 3-4 and number of client projects is projected at approximately 10-12. The Marketing and International Business Department would like to request a teaching assistant (TA) to assist with OWNERSHIP of various functions of the overall course, partnering with the instructor, to play a key role in helping create a more efficient and successful course experience, for all cross-functional partners: Students, Clients, Instructors.

Additional Description of Need:
- Some of the most fundamentally challenging aspects of the course is managing multiple projects from different clients, all with specific needs and objectives, per project
- The uniqueness of each project and client requires significant bandwidth from the instructor to help manage peculiarities while constantly synthesizing various details into more general learning for all students in the course

- The course inherently has many moving parts and fluidity
- The instructor of this course inherently doesn't have as much control over all variables, and therefore a TA that could reduce the administrative and scheduling burdens, and perhaps answer some basic questions for students, would allow more time working with students and project details

TA responsibilities:
- With support of instructor, manage calendar/scheduling of all meetings/functions between the following:
  - 1. Instructor and students; 2. Instructor, clients, and students; 3. Clients and students
  - Students and internal Baruch stakeholders (i.e., Weissman, Schwartz Center for Communication)
- Manage scheduling all due dates for all project phases and all other assignments throughout the semester

Requirements:
Hard Skills:
- Exceptional attention to detail
- Ability to be available on email communication, approximately 4-6 days per week

- Project management skills; ability to manage multiple moving parts, at times, for approximately 45-50 students and 10-12 clients
- Attending one class session, either a Tuesday or Thursday at 4:10 – 5:25 pm, approximately once or twice a month, approximately 4-8 times overall.

Soft Skills:
- Ability to manage multiple priorities and moving parts, simultaneously
- "Customer service" skills, managing diverse personalities – students and clients
- Ability to strike a balance with students by being supportive, yet firm and empowered
- Ability to digest ambiguous messages (sometimes from students) and simplifying and synthesizing, for the most efficient and beneficial outcomes, per situation
- Flexibility and ability to respond to various reasonable changes and needs from any stakeholders

Evaluation:
- Accuracy in managing all administrative and operational details of the course (dates, requests)
- Accuracy in managing any and all changes/requests from instructor, students, and clients

- Clear and effective communication of necessary info with all stakeholders on a timely basis

Budget:
$15 per hour. Approximately 140 hours for the semester. Average of 10 hours per week.

As you can see as well with this example, I've hopefully covered the six main elements I've discussed above: Summary; Problem; Rationale (Reason); Solution; Budget; Timing.

CHAPTER FIVE | THE ONE-PAGER

CHAPTER PURPOSE:
- To provide people with QUICK documents that are easier, simpler, and faster to digest.

In your careers, as well as in school (the better teachers should stress this, by the way, especially in business school), it's important to know how important brevity is.

It's always best to summarize everything on just one page, whenever possible. Even if no one specifically asks for this (and some will), it's a good idea to provide people one-pagers for basic deliverables. People will notice that you were able to make your point on only one page.

Leave all the wonderful details for another document, or if/when it's asked for.

The person reading your documents doesn't have time to read, and read, and read. Again, in business, people want to scan. And providing a one-pager makes things so much easier to absorb.

In some ways, it's difficult to "teach" how to do a one-pager, because your document can be about anything. But that gives me even more motivation to try and help you.

Think of your one-pager as a brochure. For those with a marketing/sales background or mindset, this may come a bit more naturally. But it's beneficial to all.

Actually, if you're not a marketing-minded person and can begin to embrace this, you'll turn it into an even stronger competitive advantage. And you'll stand out even further, from your peers.

A brochure (even those that are more than one page, or in pamphlet form, etc.) is meant to attract the reader in a concise way with the key points that the company thinks their audience will need and want.

In general, your one-pagers should include:

- Quick Summary
- Purpose
- Timing (General or Specific)

They may also consist of other elements. As I mentioned, it's difficult to specifically synthesize all of the permeations in a guidebook. But if you can embrace this, directionally, you'll be in pretty good shape.

While I can't offer specifics of each case, what I can offer you, STRATEGICALLY, is the thinking that goes into preparing your one-pager. I'd say think of it like this as you decide what should be in your one-pager:

What am I trying to achieve, exactly?

- Do I want to offer a summary of something?
- Am I trying to persuade or "sell" something?

If you're trying to offer a summary or something concise of something that's larger, you probably want to condense each aspect of the larger document/file while not necessarily including all of the elements and making sure that you emphasize the things that you want to make sure your reader(s) know.

If you're trying to persuade in your one-pager, and you're preparing this for your boss or other senior executives, you probably want to have these elements:

- Summary/Intro/Purpose
- Advantages/Benefits
- Challenges/Obstacles (I'd focus mainly on strategic ones, not technical)
- Application
- Timing
- Cost

Of course, not every one-pager needs to have all of these elements.

Here's an example of a more comprehensive document, followed by an abbreviated, one-pager.

I've placed the elements that I'd put in a one-pager, in bold. This original document, on standard 8.5 x 11" paper is 3 pages long. And I promise, that the one-pager version fits on one standard, 8.5" x 11" page ☺

This document is about Whole Foods, discussing strategy for at least one of "365" stores (as a start), marketing/operations issues, and positioning.

Original:
For the 365 store located in Bellevue, Washington, **the recommendations that would best gain awareness, traffic and revenue is to make the store open 24 hours a day, 7 days a week and a store that has a small footprint in square footage that also carries few SKU numbers, reduce customer service and is an express experience.**

The rationale for going 24 hours a day, 7 days a week is to offer healthy and quality food options to LOHAS (lifestyle of healthy and sustainability) consumers that **may not be able to make it to a regular Whole Foods or a competitor due to their schedules.** This part of the LOHAS consumers depend on **convenience stores that have late hours but unhealthy and low quality food options for them. 365 would be a solution to help mainly the peripheral and mid-level LOHAS attain the food they seek.**

The small footprint and fewer SKU's put 365 in direct competition with up and coming non-traditional food retailers. Since the majority of the locals are considered **hipsters, data showcases that there is a strong preference from this audience for a non-traditional food retailer format.** In 2010, convenience store format and other (mass, limited assortment, dollar, small grocery and military) made up 15.4% and 13% of the grocery market. Conventional supermarkets make up 25.6% of the market. **If we combine convenience stores and other, that puts their market share at 28.4%.** Thus, leveling out the playing field for non-traditional food retailer formats. Another example of the benefit of a smaller store is Trader Joe's. Trader Joe's has more comparative sales per square foot. **Whole Foods made approximately $800 per square foot and Trader Joe's made approximately $1,300 per square foot in 2005. But unlike Whole Foods and Trader Joe's, 365 would be 24/7. This would allow for an increased potential revenue from each square foot.**

With the integration and use of Amazon's technology and Amazon Prime in general, I would reduce the customer service part of labor and **implement express checkouts via mobile device from any food touch point.** For example, if you want to buy an apple, you go to the apple section and pay via your mobile device or card at that section. For customers with full baskets, we would also have self-checkout stations instead of cashiers. The objective is to have the consumer select their food and be able to go eat and enjoy their food at home, work or other as fast as possible. The express concept is similar to that of an urgent care. You need stitches? Do not go to the hospital and spend unnecessary time and money. Go to an urgent care clinic and get the stitches quickly and leave quickly.

Management would be impacted by having to **reset the comp set to reflect stores that have extended hours or that operate 24 hours a day, 7 days a week**. However, they should continue to track competitors such as Trader Joe's since they offer similar products at a similar price point. The other impact would be that of synchronizing and maintaining the **NFC and other point of sales software and hardware.** This goes farther than just maintaining the accuracy of product descriptions and updates. Management needs to stress the importance of cyber security to prevent any possible hacking to the software and hardware.

The financing would be impacted by the foot print size of the store as well as the **increased operating costs** (without customer service labor). With the smaller store, the property lease would be less expensive due to size, however, the location in Bellevue would probably not be in a tertiary location. This would mean that the overall cost to open the store, construction and lease, would be balanced. **The operating costs with the smaller store would** need to have a reallocation of labor costs. There will need to be an increase in restocking and inventory team members. Due to the implementation of NFC and other point of sales at various sections, customer service team members can be reduced significantly. The new technology integration is at an increased, upfront cost as well. The hardware components need to have depreciation applied.

Operations would be impacted by the need to focus on **restocking and inventory over customer service in the 365 store.** The team should be training on efficient methods of restocking as food and products begin to move from their spaces in order to maintain the perception of always being stocked and not running low or having shortages. The other impact on operations is **maintaining the physical store safe and secure during the 24 hours of operation a day.** The needs to be a sense of safety if a consumer shops the store at 3am.

365 days of quality healthy food options, now open 24 hours!

- The reason behind this positioning statement is to showcase to consumers that 365 **provides you with the food you're seeking any time of the day.**

Everything healthy, pure and raw. Everything Whole Foods.

- For Whole Foods, since they have a larger foot print with many SKU's, this positioning statement encompasses everything that they offer consumers as well as what they are.

One-pager:

Recommendations:
Bellevue, Washington 365 Store:
- Open store 24/7 to best gain awareness, traffic and revenue.
- Store has a small footprint in square footage that also carries few SKU numbers, reduce customer service and is an express experience.

Rationale:
- Offer healthy and quality food options to LOHAS (lifestyle of healthy and sustainability) consumers that may not be able to make it to a regular Whole Foods or a competitor due to their schedules.
- These LOHAS consumers depend on convenience stores that have late hours but unhealthy and low quality food options for them.

- 365 would be a solution to help mainly the peripheral and mid-level LOHAS attain the food they seek.

Supporting Info:

- Since the majority of the locals are considered hipsters, data showcases that there is a strong preference from this audience for a non-traditional food retailer format.
- In 2010, convenience store format and other (mass, limited assortment, dollar, small grocery and military) made up 15.4% and 13% of the grocery market. Conventional supermarkets make up 25.6% of the market.
- If we combine convenience stores and other, that puts their market share at 28.4%. Whole Foods made approximately $800 per square foot and Trader Joe's made approximately $1,300 per square foot in 2005. But unlike Whole Foods and Trader Joe's, 365 would be 24/7. This would allow for an increased potential revenue from each square foot.

Implications:

- With the integration and use of Amazon's technology and Amazon Prime, reduce the customer service part of labor and implement express checkouts via mobile device from any food touch point.
- Management would be impacted by having to reset the comp set to reflect stores that have

extended hours or that operate 24 hours a day, 7 days a week.

- Continue to track competitors such as Trader Joe's since they offer similar products at a similar price point.
- Synchronizing and maintaining the NFC and other point of sales software and hardware.
- Increased operating costs.
  - Increase in restocking and inventory team members.
  - Yet customer service team member costs offset, due to the implementation of NFC and other point of sales at various sections.
- Operations impacted by the need to focus on restocking and inventory over customer service in the 365 store.
- Additional operational impacts: maintaining the physical store safe and secure during the 24 hours of operation a day.

Positioning Statement:

365 days of quality healthy food options, now open 24 hours!

Showcase to consumers that 365 **provides you with the food you're seeking any time of the day.**

Again, I can't capture every example in a book. But the above elements should, in some way, cover essentially all possibilities. So choose which ones you think you need based on the objectives of what you're going to submit, and why. And I think you'll be in pretty good shape.

CHAPTER SIX | EXECUTIVE SUMMARIES

CHAPTER PURPOSE:
- To dispel the myth about executive summaries and discuss what their genuine purpose is.
- To understand how to better craft your executive summaries.

The biggest mistruth about executive summaries is that they are a summary. They are NOT summaries. Executive Summaries are:

- The foundation of the business case
- They are the sales pitch
- You're selling your solution to the client's problem

The executive summary demands a whole different approach to writing than the rest of the proposal.

It's about key information with a persuasive, well-substantiated pitch.

The executive summary must demonstrate a clear understanding of the potential client's needs.

Executive summaries should be crafted with the audience firmly in mind.

What you want to make sure of is to put the most critical information in the first few paragraphs.

Here are the elements of an executive summary:

- The Opener: Capture Their Attention
- The Need: We Understand
- The Solution: Here's the Fix
- The Evidence: How We'll Do It
- The Call to Action: Let's Do It

The Opener
You'll need an opener that's compelling. Get your client's attention right away, and you do that by talking about THEM, not about you. Once AGAIN, it's about the **audience**!

Focus on the issue and the result, but be direct, concise, and evocative.

This is the time to hook them in — get them excited about what they're going to read next.

The Need
You can't solve a problem that you don't understand. This section of the executive summary is where you demonstrate your grasp of the situation.

You could include a bit of your own research or a brief reference to your agency's experience dealing with a similar situation

You should also talk about how the client will benefit from solving the problem - what will change, the positive outcomes, the results.

The Solution
This section is where you talk about the brilliant solution you're proposing and why it will work.

But remember, this is just an overview.

They can read all the details in the proposal so keep it high level but still provide enough detail to convince them you have something specific and well thought out for them.

This section should start to provide the client with a sense of "relief" and get them excited about the result.

The Evidence
Talk about why your company, your team, or your product is not only willing to take this challenge on, but you're qualified to do so.

Maybe this is your niche market and you have lots of experience helping other companies with a similar issue.

Maybe it's a particular skill set your team possesses, your research, your algorithm, or your project management process, etc.

The Call to Action
Keeping in mind that the purpose of the executive summary is to sell, it's now time to close the deal.

Make the client feel that you differentiate from the competition and prove your solution is the one that will make their business better.

Talk about why you want to work with them — a little flattery goes a long way — and about how, as partners, you will be successful.

Here's an example of an executive summary. (Note: italics precede each section, only as an indication):

The Opener
For the past 30 years, **Client's Company** has selected fellows who have tackled some of the biggest national and global issues with innovative and transformational solutions. Your company has directly and indirectly improved the lives of millions of people all over the world. In the midst of all of the different matters in this world that need solving, we have found that there is one, very large group of people in our country that most of the time goes unnoticed: children born into poverty.

The Need

More than 1 in every 10 children in America today spend more than half of their childhood years in poverty. That amounts to over 9 million children. These children then, very often, fall into a vicious cycle of hardship and deprivation for the rest of their lives. When they become young adults, they are unlikely to finish school, thus lacking basic skills to get a job. Their children will, more than likely, follow a similar path, and the cycle begins again. Unfortunately, only a few of these children manage to defy these statistics and become economically successful. This causes both a moral and an economical problem in today's society.

The Solution

Through years of research, interviews, and hands on experience, **Your Company** has comprised a plan to fight child poverty in America, and ensure that those born into poverty end the cycle. The plan consists of four different phases, all designed to guide, support, and motivate underprivileged youths through the most important years of their lives. We will start with ensuring that these children are given the right tools to complete high school, and continue by offering consistent guidance throughout college applications, job interviews, and career exploration. Our main goal is to give these children something they may have never known was possible: options.

The Evidence

All of the founders here at **Your Company** are very passionate about this cause. That is why we have spent the past three years performing extensive research on the subject. We have studied relevant reports from the country's most prestigious sociologists, economists, and education professionals. We have conducted interviews with voluntary families, teachers, and professional experts. Over this time we have come to realize the severity of this problem and the importance of doing something about it.

The Call To Action

Client's Company has been a catalyst for positive change for so many different projects that have unquestionably changed the world. With your help, we too can make all the difference in the lives of millions of children in our country. This proposal outlines, in detail, our plan on how to do just that. **Let's change the game. Let's show millions of children that they are not a statistic.**

So what have we done here with The Opener?

Hopefully we made it about THEM, not you. And yes, we did "flatter" them a bit by making sure we knew something about them and their successes while not going too far. You don't want to go too far and provide too much info that a company already knows about themselves. Just take a few key points and share them, to help them know that you know about them. Yes, it's flattery to an extent. But this is business writing. It's about the real-world. And if done correctly, it works.

What have we done here with The Need?
We used some key statistics to show that we understand the problem. And we didn't make this section all that long and drawn out. The need is the entire point, and in most business situations, understanding the issue is about demonstrating you can pinpoint it, succinctly.

What have we done here with The Solution?
Hopefully if we've done a good job articulating the issue (need) we are now offering a clear and very strong, compelling case in why and how we can offer the solution to the problem. We've made it specific and outlined four phases. And hopefully as you can see, we are also getting them excited about it.

What have we done here with The Evidence?
Here we're showing that we've really done our homework and can back up why we're the best for the solution. We've mentioned the depth in which we've studied this issue. And we've also highlighted all of the interviews and research you've done with various, key stakeholders.

<u>What have we done here with The Call to Action?</u>
Here we're closing by once again reminding the client what is great about them and why we and the client make the best fit. Don't go overboard but finish here with something passionate (but genuine, not cheesy) that you feel will evoke their sensibilities and energize them into wanting to work with you. Here you've made an emotional plea to not allow children to become a statistic. Close by betting on something that you and your potential client care deeply about.

CHAPTER SEVEN | EMAILS

CHAPTER PURPOSE:
- To better understand how to craft your emails by better organization of what needs to be there and what doesn't.
- To understand some tactical, and sometimes basic, issues that are easy but OFTEN overlooked.

The following is a real example from a sales director of an organization (someone in their 50s, by the way) writing to the marketing manager. Sorry, but this is a very poorly written email, for various reasons.

Here's the original version (with obviously concealed names). And whatever grammatical errors there may be, they remain in there.

Kimberlie:
I've been compiling executive contacts for my target accounts. These accounts will be largely legacy accounts that have not migrated to SAP. I was hoping to get some time to understand the requirements for uploading these accounts for an outbound email and old-fashioned cold calling campaign follow up. This would include any templates format that you would use to upload these lists in the salesforce application that we have

in house. I would also be curious to know if the application you use provides the names of the companies that you may already have in the database so that I do not duplicate my efforts. If there is a list of reference data of the content for these types of campaigns we have done in the past. I would like to see if I can repurpose the information graphics etc. for my own efforts. I hope to be getting access and training for CRM to see what accounts we have identified from the past that could also be prime suspects.
Best regards,
Al

Here is how I'd probably write this email:

Hi Kimberlie:
I'd like to understand the requirements for uploading executive contacts into salesforce. (Mainly legacy accounts that haven't migrated to SAP for an outbound email and old-fashioned cold calling campaign follow up).

Curious about:
- Any templates that you would use to upload these lists in the in-house salesforce application?
- If the application you use provides the names of the companies to avoid duplication?

- Any content I can reference for these types of campaigns we have done in the past?

Best regards,

Al

Let's dissect a few issues here. And to follow some of my own advice, I put the comparison in table form.

	ORIGINAL	MY VERSION
# of Words	174	81
Discusses purpose of note immediately upfront?	No	Yes, 56% LESS words
White space?	No	Yes
Bullet points?	No	Yes
Easy to read?	No	Yes
Easier to digest?	No	Yes (Hopefully)

In addition, here are some sentences/phrases that I don't think need to be there since the recipient doesn't need to know this to answer the email. And frankly, probably doesn't care about:

- I've been compiling executive contacts for my target accounts.
- I would like to see if I can repurpose the information graphics etc. for my own efforts.
- I hope to be getting access and training for CRM to see what accounts we have identified from the past that could also be prime suspects.

TACTICAL ISSUES WITH EMAIL

CHECK YOUR SENT FOLDER

When you send emails, I recommend that you ALWAYS do a quick check and make sure that your email also shows up in your "sent" folder. I do this with every single email I send, for years. Not only business emails, but personal ones as well. Because if you send an email and it didn't transmit, then it's like you never sent it at all.

I can't tell you how many times people have told me that they thought they sent me an email but it was still in their pending box. I'm not naïve and I'm sure throughout the years that some people were just lying. But some weren't. Technology isn't perfect. Your WiFi can go out for a second while you're sending an email on your laptop. Or, since we all have email on our phones, you can lose your connection for a minute or two, etc.

EMAIL PING PONG

I was tempted to call this email tag, and some people do. But what I wanted to share here is a little more important, and why I've always called it email ping pong. Try not to engage in going back and forth with someone in email when nothing is getting accomplished or solved. I can't tell you how many "rounds" of emails you should wait until it's unhealthy. You'll need to use your sense for that.

But I'll tell you that when nothing is getting accomplished, and especially when there are other people copied on the exchanges (spectators) that makes things look really bad. Get on the phone or if you work in the same physical location, walk over to the person to resolve it.

I don't want to tell you that you're also in danger of putting things in writing that shouldn't be there; I know you already know that. And I won't insult your intelligence.

Even if what's being ping-ponged is something benign but nothing is getting solved, trust me, it looks bad. So just don't further engage and solve it by communicating another way.

SUBJECT LINES

Subject lines should always be specific as possible, for a variety of reasons. A good subject line will (hopefully) give the recipient a reason to promptly open your email.

Here are some examples where I'm first sharing a poor subject line and then an improved one.

But, there are times when a vague subject line makes sense. The most obvious reason is when there needs to be an extra level of confidentiality. Since sometimes there are others who can see the recipient's inbox.

A quick example of this might be if someone needs to unfortunately be disciplined or terminated. Or maybe you need to initiate a complaint. If you need to share information about Mike Smith, it may make more sense if the subject line simply says "MS."

There are other times where a non-descript subject line makes sense. I was once doing some consulting for a company (where I'd go to the office 2-3 times a week). And this was sometime in 2015, when there was that unfortunate terrorist attack in France.

The company I was working for was owned by a French businessman and his wife. And I knew they had many ties to France and traveled there often.

I wanted to share my empathy and say something supportive. My subject line was:

Subject: 11/13

I think based on the circumstances, this is better than writing a subject line that goes something like:

Sorry to Hear
Sorry
Are you OK?

Hopefully you see my point. Remember, even though I was reaching out on a human level, I was using corporate email to two people that I had a business relationship with, not a personal one.

CHAPTER EIGHT | WHITE SPACE

CHAPTER PURPOSE:

- To understand how to break up your emails and business messages and make them easier and faster to absorb what's necessary.
- To utilize bullet points, numbered points, headers, sub-headers, etc.

There's something that in business writing call "white space," and it's what it sounds – literally, white space.

When you embark on your careers, and even in school, the more you can adjust your style to bullet points, the MORE EFFECTIVE you'll be as a written communicator and PEOPLE WILL NOTICE and appreciate this style. Please trust me on this. You can even get some type of advantage for doing this.

Let me break this down for you by showing a progression. Take the following fictitious email I may write to a vendor in my industry:

Hi Nate:
I wanted to ask for the status of next round samples. I need to better understand what the delays are about. On the last conference call we had, we discussed the changes that design requested, how those changes were going to possibly affect the schedule and if so, by how long? I need to go back to

R&D and alert them to adjust the timelines on their end. Please get back to me asap.
Thanks,
Al

Seems like a fairly innocent, benign email, I hope? And it is. But I think there's a better way. Before I show you, let's take a look at what is important in this email, in bold:

Hi Nate:
*I wanted to ask for the **status of next round samples.** I need to better understand what the **delays** are about. On the last conference call we had, we discussed the **changes that design requested, how those changes were going to possibly affect the schedule and if so, by how long?** I need to go back to R&D and alert them to adjust the timelines on their end. Please get back to me asap.*
Thanks,
Al

So now that you can see what matters, in bold, let's try re-structuring this email with more white space and bullet points:

Hi Nate:
Need status of next round samples to better understand the delays. On the last conference call we discussed:

- *changes design requested*
- *how those changes possibly affect schedule*
- *if so, by how long?*

Need to get back to R&D and alert them to adjust timelines on their end.

Please get back to me by tomorrow after you speak with China tonight.
Thanks,
Al

I hope you can see with this latest iteration, this is easier to read. Actually, you don't want people to read your emails. No, honestly, what I just said may seem odd. But it's better to practice how to write emails so that the recipient(s) don't read emails, but instead SCAN them. They'll appreciate that.

While it's important to be mindful that many business emails are read on a mobile phone these days, and the real estate on the screen is minimal, white space and "breaking up" your overall message is critical.

BULLET POINTS, HEADERS, SUB-HEADERS

While you know what bullet points, headers, and sub-headers are, there's a good chance you're not using them. Either at all, or barely.

And if you're a student (undergrad or grad), you're probably not using them at all and you're business writing can use some help. No, really. So fix it.

You saw an example earlier in this chapter of how to take an email and re-write a good portion of it into bullet points. Let's now break it down so you can use this as a template, or guideline.

I'm not an academic, even though I've also been teaching now for 14 years. So in some ways, it's kind of simple in terms of what should convert into bullet or numbered points.

Use bullet points for the most important portions of your emails or documents; the parts you want your reader(s) to actually focus on.

Take this report written in original format; I've highlighted the areas that I think are the most important.

The public education system is under supported and underfunded in the majority of minority-immigrant communities. The lack of support creates a need for organizations like Echoing Green to fill. Partnering with an organization like Echoing Green, the same organization that originally funded City Year, would be the ultimate backbone for Starting Smart to create real change in minority-immigrant communities. Echoing Green will take pride in choosing Smarting Smart as one of their 2018 fellows.

Starting Smart will provide rigorous academic support in underserved and minority communities in New York City. Together with Echoing Green, we will transform the lives of Americans who weren't born into the upper echelons of society. The United States was built by immigrants and yet they have been forgotten. **Immigrant youth are left to develop in school systems that do not have the adequate staff or facilities to create real positive change. A program like Starting Smart will help the current generation being tutored break away from a poverty cycle and change their family tree leading to positive growth for multiple generations. College-aged children of immigrants will be able to work at Starting Smart. We will help develop their resumes by hiring them as the tutors in our supplemental education program. They will be able to work around their schedules, while contributing financial to their households which many have to do.** Teaching youth from similar backgrounds will give both individuals the confidence they need to move forward with their dreams.

Starting Smart can accomplish real change. We are inspired by City Year and believe we can follow in their footsteps for long term growth as an organization. **City Year offers supplemental education during school hours but Starting Smart will be there outside of school hours. My team has experience in program development and were City Year volunteers after graduating from college. We saw the value in educating students who might have been lost through the system anyway but knew there was something missing.**

Supplemental education shouldn't be a luxury only suited for families who can afford it. Every child in America deserves the same chance at life and to change their futures. Echoing Green is the perfect partner for us and together we will instill confidence and knowledge in the future of America.

Now let's take a look at it with bullet points to break it up:

The public education system is under supported and underfunded in the majority of minority-immigrant communities. The lack of support creates a need for organizations like Echoing Green to fill. Partnering with an organization like Echoing Green, the same organization that originally funded City Year, would be the ultimate backbone for Starting Smart to create real change in minority-immigrant communities. Echoing Green will take pride in choosing Smarting Smart as one of their 2018 fellows.

Starting Smart will provide rigorous academic support in underserved and minority communities in New York City. Together with Echoing Green, we will transform the lives of Americans who weren't born into the upper echelons of society. The United States was built by immigrants and yet they have been forgotten.

- Immigrant youth are left to develop in school systems that do not have the adequate staff or facilities to create real positive change.
- A program like Starting Smart will help the current generation being tutored break away from a poverty cycle and change their family tree leading to positive growth for multiple generations.
- College-aged children of immigrants will be able to work at Starting Smart.
- We will help develop their resumes by hiring them as the tutors in our supplemental education program.
- They will be able to work around their schedules, while contributing financial to their households which many have to do.

Teaching youth from similar backgrounds will give both individuals the confidence they need to move forward with their dreams.

Starting Smart can accomplish real change. We are inspired by City Year and believe we can follow in their footsteps for long term growth as an organization.

- City Year offers supplemental education during school hours but Starting Smart will be there outside of school hours.
- My team has experience in program development and were City Year volunteers after graduating from college.
- We saw the value in educating students who might have been lost through the system anyway but knew there was something missing.

Supplemental education shouldn't be a luxury only suited for families who can afford it. Every child in America deserves the same chance at life and to change their futures. Echoing Green is the perfect partner for us and together we will instill confidence and knowledge in the future of America.

As you can hopefully see, we've broken up the overall document by using bullet points and the concept of white space.

Just to make clear, it's not about breaking things up into bullet points for the sake of bullet points. It's not arbitrary.

It's about breaking things up that we feel are most important and necessary for our reader(s) to know into bullet points. It's similar to the email example I shared in Chapter One.

And we have a better chance at our reader absorbing the key info we want them to. I think the second version is more SCANNABLE and doesn't require as much READING.

CHAPTER NINE | STOP WRITING SO MUCH — USE TABLES, CHARTS, AND GRAPHS

CHAPTER PURPOSE:
- To rely more on visual aids more than written numbers for a variety of business reports
- To understand how to BETTER utilize tables, charts, and graphs by marrying your point to the overall visual.

In line with the overall theme about businesspeople wanting to scan and not read, I strongly recommend that you embrace tables, charts, graphs, etc. as much as possible.

I'm not going to insult your intelligence by mentioning what TYPES of info go best with each type of tactic. You can read that sort of thing on the internet if you don't already know it. Instead, I'd rather focus on doing what I do best – adding some unique comments that are hopefully a value-add to you.

I really think that most students and even some business practitioners don't really understand the point of charts and how to really use them **most effectively**.

If you really think about it, the purpose of these tools, while they present certain information in a cleaner way, is not just about presenting all of the information.

It's about making ONE main point in each chart, graph, or table that you want to bring up.

So when you present a table, chart, graph, etc., ask yourself: What is the ONE thing that I want to make sure my reader lifts off of the page?

So let's say you're offering a bar graph of 5 years' worth of market share for a particular company for a particular product. Let's say your bar graph looks something like this:

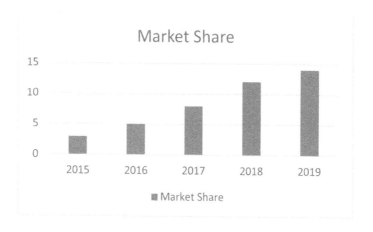

So what is your point with the above bar graph? You might be thinking, "I provided 5 years' worth of market share. That's my point."

No, sorry but that's not a point, per se. I'm sorry –
I'm being sincere. There's a pretty good chance that
the numbers, no matter what the industry or
application is, are just numbers. And not enough. So
I go back to asking, what is your point?

Maybe you want to share the annual growth rate?
Ah! That might be a point. Well, if that's the case,
then the above isn't enough. And I'd say it's stronger
if you present it this way:

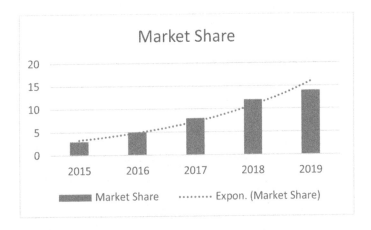

This now shows an exponential line where you can
then make a case that for the past 5 years, market
share has increased an average of almost 3% each
year.

You now have a better bar graph that supports your
point.

There are many different ways you can, DIRECTIONALLY, begin to embrace tables and charts and make your content (whether on a slide or a written business report) a lot more effective.

This doesn't mean to turn an entire PowerPoint or business report into visuals. Of course, you need analysis and commentary. Use some judgment, but take numbers and make them come to life with visuals.

A quick note for finance/accounting people: I'm a marketing guy but this advice is especially beneficial for finance/accounting people to take their data and make it more digestible, frankly.

In general, here are some quick tips on when to use which tool:

- Tables: very useful when comparing things. As well as tabulating/presenting general data.
- Charts: very useful when presenting various types of information in a variety of ways.
- Graphs: very useful when wanting to have a POWERFUL visual that takes your point and PUNCHES it to really stand out.

TABLES

Here's a simple example of taking pricing information, although already in bullet points (a good thing), which I think is more effective in a table. Notice, I'm saying *more* effective – this isn't an exercise in making things look marginally better (aesthetically). It's about effectiveness.

Let's say you've tabulated the following pricing for some categories (let's assume there will be some type of analysis afterwards but that's not important for now).

- LED devices with gel: $50 - $200
- Toothpastes: $5 - $30
- Strips and other kits: $30 - $50
- Whitening pens: $20 - $30

Why not create a simple table and instead, share your content this way?

Category	Average Price	Notes
Toothpaste	$5-30	
Strips	$30-50	
Gel Trays	$180+	Custom made
Pens	$20-30	
LED/UV	$50-200	Depends on gel solution/light

GRAPHS

Here, you can present the following information in a way that I think is easier to comprehend and by not forcing your audience (recipient) to read, they can save their bandwidth to digest your analysis (that would follow).

- The average revenue per person in the market for Beauty & Personal Care amounts to $ 234.93 in 2020.
- On average, females visit beauty salons every 4.4 weeks in 2017 offering potential to receive tooth whitening every 4.4 weeks
  - Males visit salons every 5.8 weeks in comparison

Perhaps present it this way:

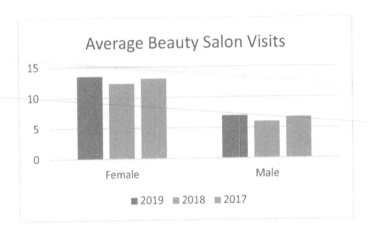

Alternatively, present it this way:

Lastly, here's a third way:

CHARTS

Charts can also be a very powerful way of presenting information. Yet at the same time, make sure you have a point. Let's say you take the following information and place it into a classic pie chart.

**Percentage of Company Revenue
By Sales**

    a) Total Company | **RM$235.5 Billion**
    b) Total Downstream Revenue | **RM$122 Billion**
    c) Downstream Revenue by Geographical Market | **RM$41.7 Billion**
    d) Disaggregation of Petrochemicals Revenue | **RM$19.1 Billion**

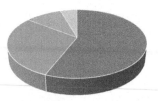

Sales

- Total Company
- Total Downstream
- By Geographical Market
- Petrochemicals Revenue

So you've placed this info in a pie chart and it does look a lot better than in list form. But, what is the point you're trying to make? That's where I think a good number of people can better understand how to be more effective.

Perhaps you're trying to make a point out of one or two segments of the business, in comparison to the whole?

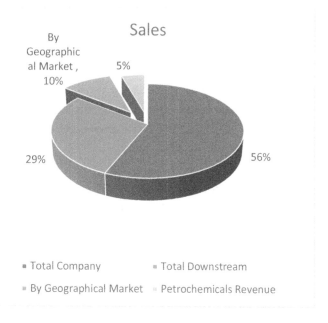

Perhaps you want to make a specific point about the 10 and 5%, geographical and petrochemical, respectively? And you now have broken up the pie chart and emphasized those two slices. And you're now in a better position to have your graphics help aid your overall point.

CHAPTER TEN | USE DECKS INSTEAD OF REPORTS

CHAPTER PURPOSE:
- To embrace using decks instead of "classic" reports wherever and whenever possible.

In your business life, I'd recommend doing away with writing "reports" as often as possible. By the way, I'm fully aware that some industries and companies still want/need things in report form. So in those cases, do the report.

But in all other cases, do your best to move away from using programs such as Microsoft Word (or whatever that free Google software is called...Google Docs maybe, something like that, they call it). Yes, even though this book was written with Word ☺

People don't want to open an email attachment and have a Word document appear. **It's a big turn off**.

One of the best lessons I've learned in business (writing) communications is to utilize decks a lot more than reports.

A deck is essentially a "report" but done in PowerPoint. It's NOT a PowerPoint presentation! Check out my book on Presentation skills for advice on that.

A deck (as opposed to a PowerPoint presentation file) has more words and more detail included, but it's at the same time a lot more "reader-friendly" and so much easier to digest.

Here's an example of a deck after returning from an overseas sourcing trip and needing to provide people in the company a download of your trip. Now, remember, you haven't been asked to present this. This is simply a download that you'll email to people.

Vendor X Download
December 2,4 & 5, 2010

Attendees:
C. McXXXXX
H. MuXXXXX
T. ThXXXXXX
A. Golzari
Vendor X Team

Agenda

- China Factory
- Factory tour
- Review Best-in-Class model
- Review

2

Innovation

- Work on seeing prototype/info on XXX and other exploratory projects
- Review device archive to look for leverage opportunities
- Review Deco strategies/bring samples. (Electroplating, water decal, etc)
- Discuss any new innovations (products, techniques/delivery methods) that may be consistent with our home fragrance strategy and product portfolio

Quality/Manufacturing

- Assess quality certifications/best practices
- Discuss better/faster/more accurate sampling procedures
- Resources allocated? Do they have model makers/sample makers?
- Leverage XXX off-shore staff better
- Understand degree of vertical integration
- Review OT & C and vendor scorecard

3

Speed/Agility

- Discuss ability to impact timing as it relates to speed end-to-end
- Tooling capabilities/processes in relation to speed (tool shop visit)
- Discuss timing for delivery/support Ops and other cross-functional teams regarding pack-out, quality, etc.
- Do you have your own, in-house best-in-practice speed model?
- What can we do to help you help us with our speed model?

Costing

- Drill down on best cost for XXX (core and novelty) as well as XXX
- Re-engineering of XXX electronic components for simplicity and lower cost
- Review plastic materials – leverage raw material opportunities related to UL standards

4

Novelty Wallflower Heater Speed Proposal – From 37 wks to 24 wks (PIF to DC)

Novelty WF Speed Opportunities

Tighter Coordination & Faster Decision-Making/Handoff – Brand/Design/bA/GSL
- Brand partnership for shorter design/color approval timing and handoff
- Align clearly at 2D & 3D on Design direction (cut down add'l time driven by design interpretations & iterations)

Testing –
- UL testing time is currently the longest hard constraint on timing at 8 wks
- QA is in process of quoting test requirements with ETL instead of UL for improved timing – TBD

Tooling & Sampling –
- Build Aluminum "Soft" Tool concurrently w/Production Tool – reduces tooling time from 6 to 3 wks to enable earlier submission for UL (or ETL) testing – est $6k/tool
- Explore new vendors with in-house tooling capabilities to shorten total Tooling time (including transit)

Transportation –
- Ocean transit with team-driver trucks (vs. Rail) for ground portion to save 1 wk – $2500/container
- Air-ship to save 2 wks – $0.40/unit incremental cost

Notes:
*PDM: foam density model. **T1: first shot sample out of a tool. ***Assumes full 8 wks of UL Testing

5

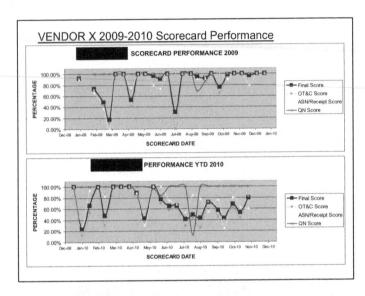

VENDOR X 2009-2010 Scorecard Performance

SCORECARD PERFORMANCE 2009

PERFORMANCE YTD 2010

VENDOR X 2010 YTD Scorecard Feedback

VENDOR	METRIC TYPE	METRIC WEIGHT	2009 AVG	2010 AVG	TREND	GREEN (>95%)	YELLOW (>90%)	RED (<90%)
XXX	FINAL SCORE	100%	85.92%	68.73%	DOWN	6	0	17
XXX	OT&C SCORE	70%	83.83%	62.88%	DOWN	6	0	17
XXX	ASN SCORE	20%	87.10%	75.88%	DOWN	7	1	15
XXX	QN SCORE	10%	98.21%	95.36%	DOWN	20	0	3

1. Poor performance from XXX so far in 2010 with scores all over the place. XXX is perhaps the only vendor who is in RED on all metrics and is down significantly from 2009. XXX must improve its scores immediately and provide a performance improvement plan to XXX. This kind of performance will not be tolerated in the future
   Average 2010 score : 68.73 (YTD, 23 scorecard runs) - RED
   - **2010 OTC (based on ASNs) score: 62.88% - RED**
   - **2010 ASN Compliance score: 75.88% - RED**
   - **2010 Quality score: 95.36% - RED**
2. OT&C is one of the lowest amongst its peers with overall score just above 60% and 3/4th of the scores in RED for 2010. This is a serious concern especially given the fact that overall scores are down more than 20% from 2009 and XXX was asked to achieve the 95% goal in 2010
3. ASN compliance has suffered as well in 2010 with overall average just above 75% and 2/3rd of scores in RED.
4. Overall quality is also in RED with a few big QNs issued in 2010.
5. Next Steps
   - Provide an action plan ASAP for scorecard and process improvement. Target should be 95% with no exceptions

96

I would put these two slides in an appendix (and see last chapter of this book):

PRODUCT X Profile

	VENDOR
LOCATION	•Shenzhen, China (South) •Shanghai (North)
Existing / New Vendor	Existing
Total FOB Cost	$1.05
WEEKLY OUTPUT	50,000 per 4 cavity tool
MAJOR CUSTOMERS	XXX
PRODUCTS PRODUCED	XXX
IN-HOUSE FACILITIES	Plastic injection, Electronic PCBA, Assembly/Pack-out
In House Tooling/Model Making	No
In house Deco	Pad Printing
Timeline 1st production	Present-state
Tooling Cost	PENDING

6

PRODUCT Y Profile

Facility Location	Mason City, IA Dongguan, China
Existing / New Vendor	Existing
Landed Cost	$1.64
Production Lead Time	4 weeks
Advantage	Speed (US lead time includes final assembly with gel packs)
Capacity (initial)	50,000 per week, per tool
Timeline for 1st production	Present-state
Tooling Costs	$20,000

7

I didn't show you anything mind shattering here. But business isn't mind shattering (it's not). And doesn't need to be. Hopefully you'll agree; the above, as PowerPoint slides, is much easier to review and digest. As opposed to placing this info in a more classic, report in Word. You don't need the classic rules of writing or English grammar, etc. You just need to clearly present the info you need to, in slides. Clean and concise is the goal here.

I completely understand, in case you're wondering, that there are way too many words here on each slide. And consult my book on presentation skills, where I drive this point home, as well. But remember, this is NOT a PowerPoint presentation. It's a deck. Decks are not the same as presentations, even though you may be using PowerPoint or Keynote to create them. Decks replace more traditional reports that are written in Word, etc.

CHAPTER ELEVEN | EMBRACE AN APPENDIX

CHAPTER PURPOSE:

- To take advantage of using an appendix or appendices instead of feeling the need to place everything within the body of your business report.
- To better understand what type of info should go in the body of your report vs. the appendix.

You all know what an appendix is. But I'm including this quick chapter since I notice people aren't using them nearly enough, or almost not at all.

And I realize I made a conscious decision to not have an appendix in this book since the details I've provided in various chapters are instructional and directly germane to the chapters (I have two appendices in my presenting book).

Using an appendix is a great way to take information that is valuable, but too detail-oriented, in its own place so that it doesn't interfere with your main points.

I know it can sometimes be a bit difficult to decipher what should go into an appendix, and what I exactly mean by "details." But with practice, it gets easier.

In a nutshell, the appendix should include all of the SUPPORTING details that are useful to the reader(s) but not necessary, at the moment, to make your point. In other words, if the info was included in the body of your document, it could be a possible distraction.

Actually, in the chapter on decks that precedes this, I suggested placing two of the slides in an appendix; the product profile slides. The reason is because the deck is mainly about the sourcing trip and more pressing matters such as production and sourcing issues, etc. The product profiles are important as supporting info but not central to the main purpose of the deck. And why I placed them in an appendix.

Let's start with a super quick, basic example, and I'll expand it for you a little further on.

Let's say I'm doing a business analysis on Mercedes-Benz's brand strategy and portfolio. One of my key points might be that while Mercedes-Benz is not shying away from four door sedans like many American brands, there does seem to be an emphasis in shifting to SUVs. But they're also launching new cross-overs as part as their overall strategy.

While I know this example doesn't have the overall context, if you wanted to share some detailed information on each of the new cross-over vehicles, you'd be better off placing them in an appendix. (And of course, simply state in the body of your document to see appendix for details on each model, etc.)

Now, if there is a key detail that supports your entire point and is central to ALL of the various Mercedes-Benz SUV models, I'd say that would be information that goes in the body of your analysis and not in the appendix.

I'd also put all of my background information in an appendix. Most of the information that would be considered "general" should go in an appendix, along with supporting info.

For example, some people have a tendency to put all types of general information about a company in some type of "intro" section. In business, that's generally not a good idea. Place the required info in the body but only to the extent its necessary. All of the rest of the general info can go in the appendices.

Take a look at the following example:

Let's say you're doing a report that's ultimately about the US market but you've also looked at other countries for key insights to help you better understand opportunities in the US market.

So you've also looked at the UK market and in the body of your report, here's some of the info you've shared:

Market Share/Trends

- Whitening toothpaste is the largest whitening product
- Whitening toothpaste also the most sold type of toothpaste, overall
- Brand X is by far the leading toothpaste brand, making the brand already known for teeth whitening
- Revenue for beauty treatments overall in the UK is increasing

Consumer Beauty Behavior

- Revenue for Beauty Salons and Hairdressers was GBP 8.6 million in 2019
- The average revenue per capita in the market for Beauty & Personal Care is predicted to be $ 234.93 in 2020.
- On average, females visit beauty salons every 4.4 weeks in 2017 offering **potential** to receive tooth whitening every 4.4 weeks
  - Males visit salons every 5.8 weeks in comparison
- Tooth whitening could be **combined** with facial, tanning, hair removal, manicure/pedicure services
- Within the past years, illegal whitening locations are also seeing an increase in

visitors showing increased demand for tooth
whitening services

OK, so here's info that I would put in an appendix
that would SUPPORT the info above, but doesn't
need to be in the body of your report:

APPENDIX:

UK Market
KPIs
- In 2018, value sales of oral care in the UK grew by
  4% to reach GBP1.3 billion
- Oral care is expected to grow at a current value
  CAGR (Compound Annual Growth Rate) of
  averaging 6% from 2018-2023 year-to-year over
  the forecast period to reach GBP 1.75 billion in
  2023
- Second largest Oral care market in western
  Europe
- 58% of households in the UK are in the middle-
  income/middle-class group (2018)
- Oral care in the UK is strongly increasing
  - Education on oral hygiene boosts the
    category which offers introductions into
    whitening products
- Toothpaste is the biggest oral hygiene market
  segment and Brand X is leading within that
  category
  - 20,935 people use a whitening toothpaste
    in the UK out of a survey answered by
    24,191

- Brand X owns second highest market share in the oral hygiene market, very close to Brand Y (0.1% difference)

I sincerely hope this helps with understanding the type of info that might be better suited in an appendix.

*It's important to acknowledge that I used the above toothpaste/whitening example from a report that was written by some of my now former students. I helped them craft what should be in an appendix and hope they're OK with my use of their example.

Please subscribe to my YouTube channel: Al Golzari

Check out my videos on presentation skills, business writing, and many more topics.

Send in comments and questions and I'll answer them in an upcoming Q&A video. And you'll get a **chance to win** a paperback copy of my <u>presentation skills</u> book:

It's Called Presenting, Not Talking Out Loud: A Quick, Strategic Guide to Effective Presentations.

Al Golzari is a senior-level consumer product professional with 15+ years' experience in product development, innovation, sourcing, and vendor management along with 10+ years of adjunct teaching experience at all levels, including executive MBA. He has worked at various companies including LBrands, Target, and Macy's, along with consulting work.

A native of northern New Jersey, he currently resides in New York City.

Made in the USA
Coppell, TX
14 July 2021

58939621R20059